THIS BOOK
BELONGS TO:

_____

TO THE GROWN-UP READER

This is a very different kind of children's book about sex.

Most books about sex are full of answers. Answers can be helpful and reassuring, but they also tell us what to think and even how to think instead of encouraging us to think for ourselves and to honor our own knowledge and experience.

Most books about sex focus only on reproduction and intercourse. You'll find neither of these topics in our book. (*What Makes a Baby*, the first book in this series, geared to younger readers, is about reproduction. The next book, for older kids, will include information on intercourse).

Sex education is about more than science and the so-called facts of life. I believe the most important part of sex education is exploring and sharing our feelings, values, and beliefs, and helping kids connect what they learn to their communities, histories, families, and cultures.

That's what this book allows you to do. We've provided the framework and basic information about bodies, gender, and touch, and we've left blanks that only you and the kids in your life can fill in.

The truth is that sex IS a funny word, but it's also a complicated one, so meaningful conversations about sex might not always feel easy or fun, but having them prepares all of us for life as it is. *Sex Is a Funny Word* is here to help.

HOW TO USE THIS BOOK

This book is meant to be read over weeks, months, and years, rather than just a few sittings. You'll find that it sparks different conversations at different ages and stages.

Before you read the book with children, or give it to children to read on their own, read it through yourself. Pay attention to the question pages at the ends of each chapter.

Think through your own answers or responses to those questions, and think about how you would address those questions with a child.

This is especially important for the last chapter in Section 4, called "Secret Touch," which deals with sexual abuse. This is a difficult topic for all of us. We don't want to imagine our children being sexually victimized, and many of us have our own experiences of sexual harassment and violence, which we can't help but bring to mind when thinking about the safety of children in our lives. Read over this chapter carefully before reading with a young person, and give yourself time and permission to respond on your own before you try to read it with a child.

Throughout the book, when you reach a question page, share your answers. If the children you are reading with aren't ready to share their own, don't pressure them. If you are patient and make room for kids to choose when to talk, eventually they will.

UNIQUE FEATURES OF THIS BOOK

FUN AND INTERACTIVE! Every chapter begins with a comic and ends with a question page or activity page. If kids want to skip ahead, let them. There's always time to go back later.

JARGON FREE! We avoid using terminology and identity labels whenever possible to make room for the different ways we describe ourselves. But we've also offered a glossary in the back of the book with words that can be hard to explain.

NO PRESSURE! The only sexual activity in this book is masturbation (in "Touching Yourself," Section 4). We'll address more behaviors in the last book in this series.

Sex Is a Funny Word was written and illustrated based on hundreds of conversations with children, parents, families, and professionals. We've included more resources and tips on talking with kids about sex in a free Reader's Guide, which is available at www.corysilverberg.com. Our work is always made richer through feedback, and we welcome your comments and questions. Thanks for reading!

— **CORY SILVERBERG**, New York City

SEX
IS A FUNNY
WORD

TEXT
© 2015 Cory Silverberg

ILLUSTRATIONS
© 2015 Fiona Smyth

PUBLISHED BY
Seven Stories Press

**LIBRARY OF CONGRESS CATALOGING-IN-
PUBLICATION DATA**

Silverberg, Cory, author.

   Sex is a funny word : a book about
bodies, feelings, and YOU / by Cory
Silverberg & Fiona Smyth.

   pages cm

   Summary: "A comic book for kids
that includes children and families of
all makeups, orientations, and gender
identities, Sex Is a Funny Word is
an essential resource about bodies,
gender, and sexuality for children
ages 7 to 10 as well as their parents
and caregivers. Much more than
the "facts of life" or "the birds and
the bees," Sex Is a Funny Word opens
up conversations between young
people and their caregivers in a way
that allows adults to convey their
values and beliefs while providing
information about boundaries, safety,
and joy. The eagerly anticipated
follow up to Lambda-nominated What
Makes a Baby, from sex educator Cory
Silverberg and artist Fiona Smyth,
Sex Is a Funny Word reimagines "sex
talk" for the twenty-first century."--
Provided by publisher.

   ISBN 978-1-60980-606-4 (hardcover)

   1. Sex instruction for children. 2. Sex
differences--Juvenile literature. 3. Sex
(Biology)--Juvenile literature. I. Smyth,
Fiona, author. II. Title.

   HQ53.S55 2015
   613.9071--dc23

   2012935181

BOOK DESIGN
Zab Design & Typography

For more information visit
www.corysilverberg.com

CORY AND FIONA WANT TO THANK
The children, parents, and
professionals who spent hours, days,
and months reading and offering
thoughts. This book is so much more
because of what you shared with us.

Cory also wants to thank
Zoë & Sadie.

Fiona wants to thank Craig.

Printed in Malaysia

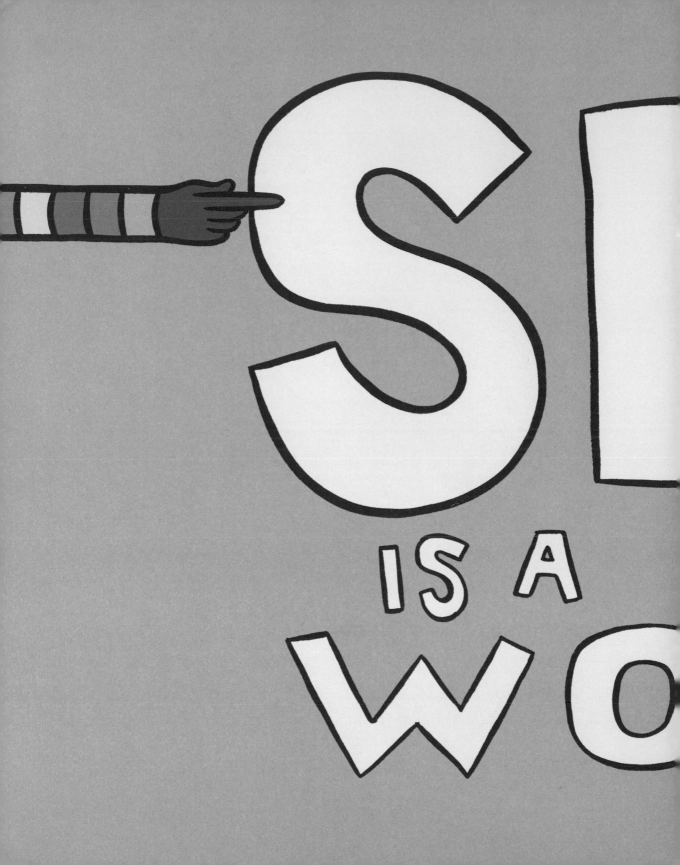

BY **CORY SILVERBERG** AND **FIONA SMYTH**

EX

FUNNY

RD

SEVEN STORIES PRESS NEW YORK | OAKLAND

Sex is a funny word.

Everyone has their own idea
of what sex is.

Some people think they don't know
anything about sex.

Some people think they know it all.

All of us
have questions about sex.

And all of us
have answers too.

13

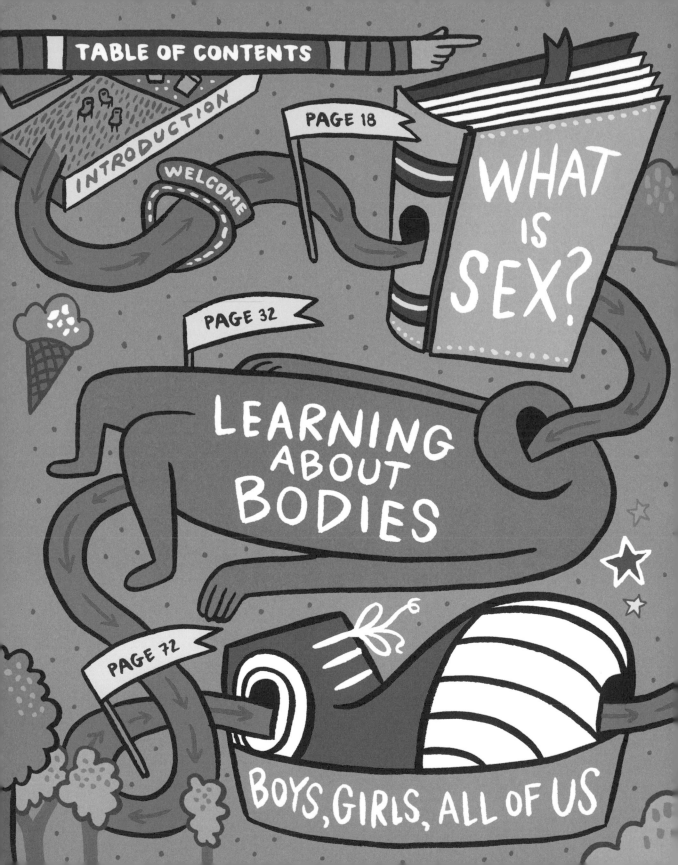

The first thing you should know about sex is that it's a word.

Some words always mean the same thing (like sunshine or crayon). Other words have many different meanings (like play).

Play can mean a show that you put on a stage, but it is also something we all do.

You might like to play sports or video games. You might sing, play an instrument, or make art.

You might play by yourself, with someone
in your family, or with friends.

How you like to play and what you play
depends on who you are. It also depends
on where you grew up, who is in your family
and community, and much more.

Sex is a word like play.
It has many meanings.

23

2. SEX IS SOMETHING PEOPLE CAN DO TO FEEL GOOD IN THEIR BODIES, AND ALSO TO FEEL CLOSE TO ANOTHER PERSON. (GROWN-UPS CALL THIS "HAVING SEX")

3. SEX IS ONE WAY GROWN-UPS MAKE BABIES. (ALSO CALLED REPRODUCTION)

If you want to learn about sex, there are a few other words that can help. Some might be new to you, and others you may already know.

Turn the page to find out what they are.

RESPECT

Treating others with respect means thinking of their feelings and the things that are important to them.

Respect goes two ways: people should respect you, and you should respect them.

IF YOU'RE READING THIS BOOK WITH SOMEONE ELSE, ONE WAY TO BE RESPECTFUL IS TO ASK BEFORE SKIPPING AHEAD.

TRUST

When you trust someone, it means you feel safe and comfortable with that person. Trusting people means knowing you can count on them. It takes time to learn who you can trust.

You can also trust yourself. Some of us know what this feels like and some of us have to learn. Nobody knows more about you than you do.

Because sex is something very personal, it's good to talk about it with people you can trust—people you are comfortable with and feel safe around.

WHEN ANSWERING QUESTIONS IN THIS BOOK, SHARE YOUR ANSWERS WITH PEOPLE YOU TRUST.

JOY

Joy is a big, beautiful, happy feeling. There are lots of ways to feel joy.

Part of sex is feeling joy and pleasure.

When you are younger, you can feel this joy and pleasure on your own, in your own body. As you get older, you might also decide to share those feelings with someone who deserves your trust.

YOU CAN FEEL JOY READING THIS BOOK BY LETTING YOURSELF LAUGH AT THE THINGS YOU THINK ARE SILLY, AND SHARING THOSE LAUGHS WITH THE PERSON YOU ARE READING WITH.

JUSTICE

Justice is like fairness, only bigger.

Justice means working together so that everyone can share in the good and the hard parts of living.

Justice means that every person and every body matters.

WHEN READING THIS BOOK, JUSTICE MIGHT MEAN STOPPING AT THE END OF EACH CHAPTER TO TALK ABOUT HOW DIFFERENT PEOPLE MIGHT THINK OR FEEL ABOUT WHAT'S IN THIS BOOK, AND HOW THAT IS DIFFERENT FROM WHAT YOU THINK AND FEEL ABOUT IT.

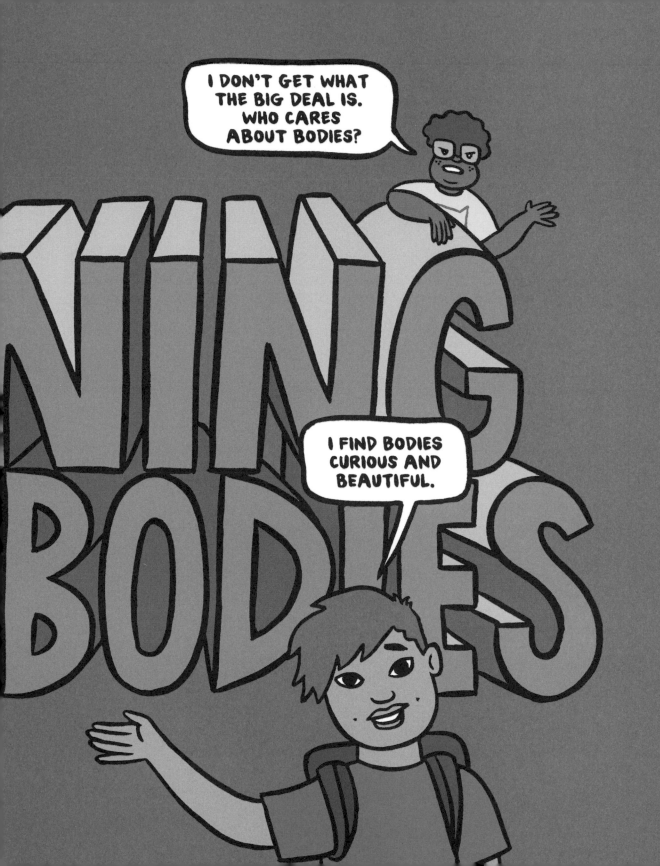

Has anyone ever told you that you can't judge a book by its cover?

It means you can't tell what's inside a book if all you know is what it looks like on the outside.

Bodies are kind of like books.

Each of us has an outside, like the cover of a book, which other people can see.

And each of us has an inside, like the inside of a book, filled with stories that only you can see and feel.

Growing up can mean learning about your outside, what your body can and can't do.

Growing up can also mean learning about your inside: the stories, memories, experiences, and feelings that make you who you are.

ME- VOLUME 7

ME- VOLUME 8

ME- VOLUME 9

EUREKA!

THE ANSWER IS IN YOUR QUESTION: IT'S MY BODY.

YEAH, THAT'S RIGHT.

THAT'S VERY AMUSING, MIMI. IT REMINDS ME OF THE RIDDLE OF THE SPHINX....

It can be fun to pay attention to how your body grows and changes.

Draw a picture of what your body looks like now. Show the parts you like the best.

Next, draw a picture of what you imagine your body could look like when you are older. Will some things look different? Will some things look the same?

CURLY HAIR

ME AGE 7

BIG feet

LAWYER

ME AGE 25

LONG HAIR AND LONG LEGS

HOW HAS YOUR BODY GROWN AND CHANGED SINCE YOU WERE A BABY?

HOW DO YOU FEEL ABOUT YOUR BODY GROWING AND CHANGING?

45

46

We are all born naked. But as soon as we're born, someone puts clothes on us.

It might start with a diaper or a blanket. Later we get pants, shirts, sweaters, dresses, jackets, gloves, and more.

There are times, like when we are having a bath or changing our clothes, when we are completely naked. Grown-ups also call this being nude.

Some people love the feeling of being naked. When you are naked you can see and touch your body without clothes getting in the way.

You can also notice how your body is changing as it grows.

Every family and community has its own rules about being naked.

Even grown-ups have to follow the rules other people make for them about when it's okay to be naked and when it isn't.

NO SHIRT
NO SHOES
NO
SERVICE

Restaurant

48

Keeping something private means
it's just for you.

You might choose to share it with
people you trust, but if it is private,
it should be your choice.

At home, the bathroom might be a private place. It's just you, and maybe someone who is there to help you.

Most people knock before going into the bathroom because it is a private place, and knocking is a way to respect privacy.

Our bodies are private too.

There are some parts we show people and other parts we cover with clothes. There are some parts that we choose to let other people touch and other parts that are just for us.

Which parts we show and which parts we keep private depends on many things like our communities and families, how old we are, and who we are sharing with.

Some people use the term *private parts* to describe parts of the body that have to do with sex.

Because any part of your body can be private, in this book we don't call them your private parts.

We call them your middle parts, because they are in the middle part of your body.

Just because we choose to keep our middle parts private and covered most of the time doesn't mean they are bad. Our middle parts are beautiful. After all, they are parts of our bodies.

56

It's good to know something about all body parts: the parts you have already, the parts you don't have yet that will grow later, and even the body parts you might never have.

You may have noticed that people don't talk about middle parts as much as they do other body parts. You may have heard different names for these parts. You may have your own name for middle parts. Sometimes people make up funny or silly names for middle parts.

Silly names can be fun, but it's also good to know the names that a teacher, doctor, or nurse would use if they wanted to tell you something or ask you a question about your body.

New beach
nudist colony

Learning about these body parts
might make you want to see them
on other people.

It's okay to be curious and want to
learn, but if someone has part of
their body covered, it's probably for
a reason. Respecting them means
not trying to see something they
don't want to show you.

But what if you're curious and want to learn? One way to do this is to look in a book with drawings. Like this one.

On the next few pages you'll find lots of drawings of middle parts. It's okay to look and ask questions when reading this book. After all, that's what this book is for.

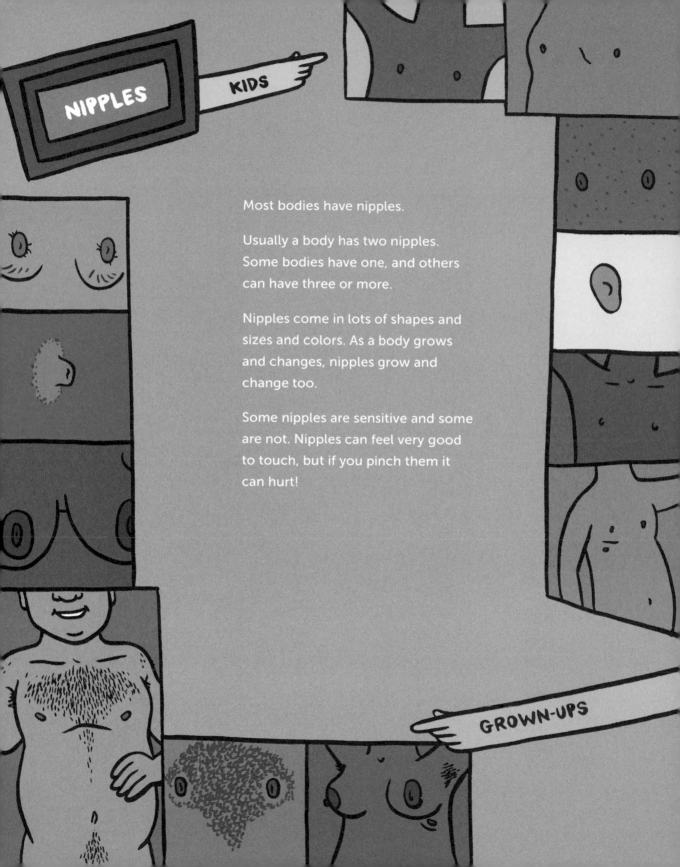

NIPPLES

KIDS

Most bodies have nipples.

Usually a body has two nipples. Some bodies have one, and others can have three or more.

Nipples come in lots of shapes and sizes and colors. As a body grows and changes, nipples grow and change too.

Some nipples are sensitive and some are not. Nipples can feel very good to touch, but if you pinch them it can hurt!

GROWN-UPS

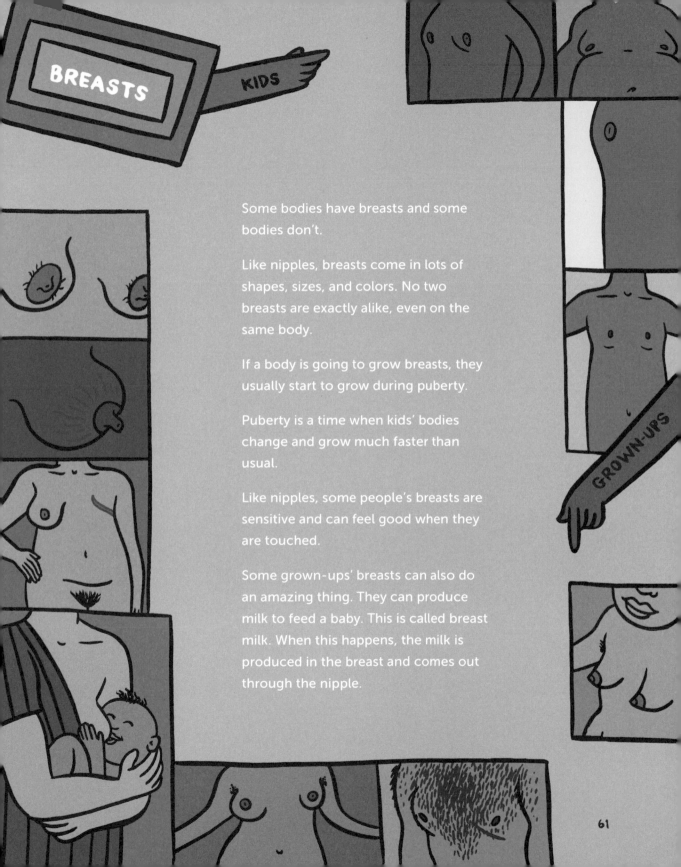

BREASTS

KIDS

GROWN-UPS

Some bodies have breasts and some bodies don't.

Like nipples, breasts come in lots of shapes, sizes, and colors. No two breasts are exactly alike, even on the same body.

If a body is going to grow breasts, they usually start to grow during puberty.

Puberty is a time when kids' bodies change and grow much faster than usual.

Like nipples, some people's breasts are sensitive and can feel good when they are touched.

Some grown-ups' breasts can also do an amazing thing. They can produce milk to feed a baby. This is called breast milk. When this happens, the milk is produced in the breast and comes out through the nipple.

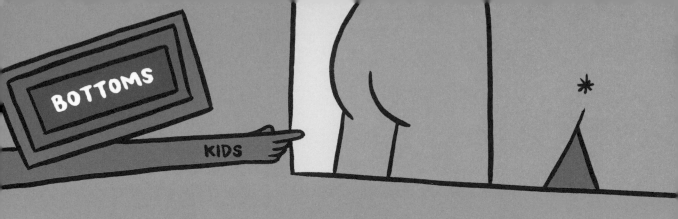

Every body has a bottom. There are lots of names people use to talk about the bottom: bum, rear end, behind, butt (which is short for buttocks), and more.

Every bottom is a little bit different in size and shape and color. As a body grows, the bottom grows too.

Bottoms have two cheeks that are soft, and most of the time we sit on them.

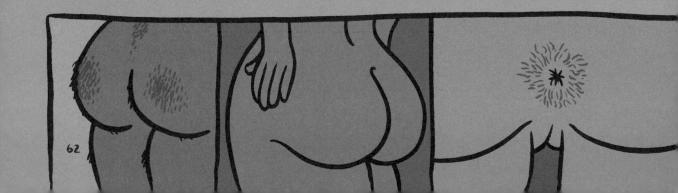

Between the cheeks, there is a hole or opening where poo (also called feces) comes out. This hole is called the anus.

Like other holes in the body, the anus is usually very sensitive, which means it can feel good to touch but can also hurt if we are rough with it.

Because the anus is where the outside of our body meets the inside, and because it is where poo comes out, we need to wash our hands after touching it.

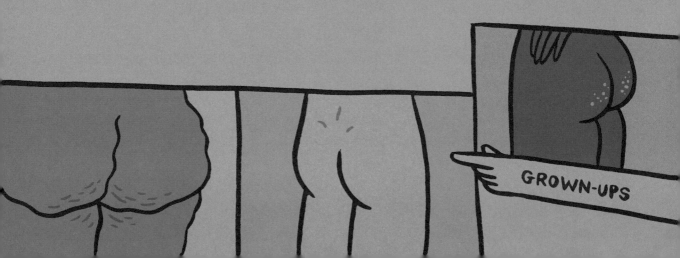

GROWN-UPS

Vulva

Some bodies have a vulva and some bodies don't.

Lots of people (including grown-ups) confuse the vulva with another middle part, the vagina. The vagina is on the inside of the body, and the vulva is on the outside.

If you have a vulva, it is the middle part between your legs that you can see.

The vulva is made of folds of skin called labia. There are many folds of skin, but when a body is young, it looks like two folds pressed together with a line down the middle.

When a body is young most vulvas look similar. As a body grows and changes, the vulva grows and changes too. During puberty, it is common for hair to grow around the vulva. Every grown-up vulva will look different.

The vulva covers and protects three other middle parts.

Clitoris

The clitoris is a middle part that is both inside and outside the body. The clitoris can be very sensitive, and touching it can feel warm and tingly.

Some clitorises are bigger than others. Some are easy to see and feel, and some are not.

The smallest part of the clitoris is on the outside of the body at the top of the vulva, where the two sides meet. This part is often hidden under a little hood. But the clitoris is much bigger than that. Most of the clitoris is inside the body, so you can't see it.

Vagina

The vagina is a middle part inside the body. The vagina is a strong and stretchy tube. There is a hole or opening to the vagina behind the vulva.

Urethra

The urethra is a small tube that has a hole or opening at one end where pee (which is also called urine) comes out. Because the urethra connects the inside of our body to the outside, it's good to wash our hands before and after we touch it.

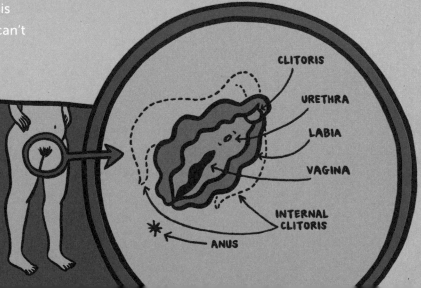

CLITORIS
URETHRA
LABIA
VAGINA
INTERNAL CLITORIS
ANUS

Penis

Some bodies have a penis and some bodies don't.

The penis is a part that sticks out, which makes it easy to see. Sometimes it is soft and sometimes it gets hard.

Like nipples, vulvas, and bums, penises come in lots of different shapes, sizes, and colors.

As the body grows, the penis will grow too. They grow the most during puberty, when hair will usually begin to grow around them.

Like the clitoris, the penis can be very sensitive, and touching it can feel warm and tingly.

Inside the penis is a small tube. This is the urethra. The tube has a hole or opening that usually ends at the tip of penis, where pee (also called urine) comes out.

Because the urethra connects the inside of our body to the outside, it's good to wash our hands before and after we touch it.

66

Foreskin

If a baby is born with a penis, there will usually be a layer of skin that covers the end of the penis like a hood. This is called the foreskin.

When a body is young, the foreskin may be tight and not move a lot. As a body grows, the foreskin loosens and grows too. It's important not to pull on the foreskin too hard before it loosens on its own.

Some families choose to have the foreskin removed, usually soon after a baby is born. This is called circumcision.

Just like every vulva looks different, so does every penis.

Scrotum and Testicles

The scrotum looks kind of like a little bag or sac that is against the body below the penis. The scrotum holds and protects the testicles (which some people call balls). Most bodies with testicles have two of them. But some have one.

The testicles are very sensitive and delicate, which is why they are protected inside the scrotum. Even with the scrotum, the testicles can be hurt if they are touched roughly.

GROWN-UPS

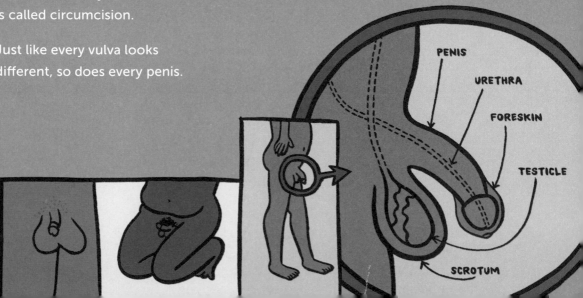

PENIS

URETHRA

FORESKIN

TESTICLE

SCROTUM

ERECTIONS

Most bodies get erections, but they only happen in certain parts of your body.

If your body has a penis, you might have noticed that sometimes it is soft and bendy, and sometimes it gets hard and doesn't bend. When it's hard and doesn't bend, that's an erection.

If your body has a clitoris, you might have noticed that sometimes it feels soft, and sometimes it feels a bit harder or firmer. When it's harder or firmer, that's an erection.

Erections can happen when we touch ourselves to feel good, but they also happen at other times: during the night when we are asleep, and first thing in the morning when we get up. Erections happen even if we're not doing anything at all. Babies will often get erections when they have to pee.

One way to think about erections is that they are just your body's way of exercising on its own.

ERECTIONS AREN'T JUST FOR BODIES. DID YOU KNOW THE WORD ERECT JUST MEANS TO MAKE SOMETHING STAND UP? WHEN A BUILDING IS BEING BUILT, THEY SAY THEY ARE ERECTING IT.

WHO HAS WHAT

Now that you know more about the middle parts, you might be curious about who has which part. After all, we keep these parts covered, so you can't tell just by looking at a person.

Most boys are born with a penis and scrotum, and most girls are born with a vulva, vagina, and clitoris.

But having a penis isn't what makes you a boy. Having a vulva isn't what makes you a girl.

The truth is much more interesting than that!

EXCELLENT QUESTION, ZAI. IF EVERYBODY IS DIFFERENT, HOW COULD THERE BE ONLY TWO KINDS OF PEOPLE?
GIRLS
FUS
WAIT, WHAT?

Once upon a time...

—actually, everywhere and all
the time, babies are born.

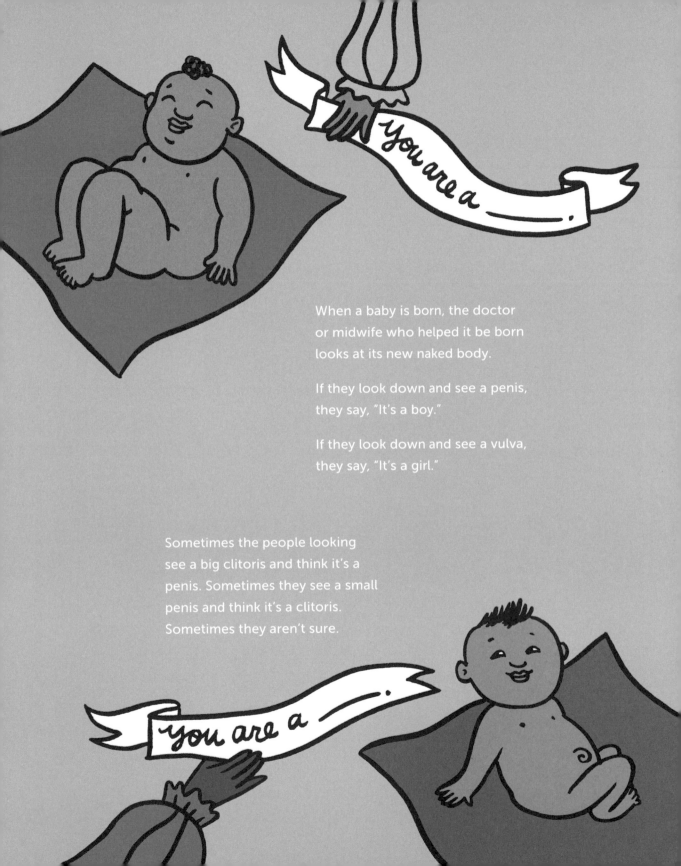

When a baby is born, the doctor
or midwife who helped it be born
looks at its new naked body.

If they look down and see a penis,
they say, "It's a boy."

If they look down and see a vulva,
they say, "It's a girl."

Sometimes the people looking
see a big clitoris and think it's a
penis. Sometimes they see a small
penis and think it's a clitoris.
Sometimes they aren't sure.

There are more than two kinds of bodies,
but they call the baby a boy or a girl
based on what they see.

This might sound like the end of the
story, but really, it's just the beginning.

When we are born, a doctor or midwife calls us boy or girl because of what we look like on the outside. They choose a word or label (usually boy or girl, or male or female) to describe our bodies.

But that's based on our outside, our cover, and who *they* think we are.

What about our whole body, inside and out? What about who *we* think we are?

As we grow into being a kid and then an adult, we get to figure out who we are and what words fit best.

Most boys grow up to be men, and most girls grow up to be women.

But there are many ways to be a boy or a girl. And there are many ways to grow up and become an adult.

For most of us, words like boy and girl, or man and woman, feel okay, and they fit. For some of us, they don't.

Maybe you're called a boy but you know you're a girl. You know how girls are treated and what they do. That's how you want to be treated and what you want to do.

Maybe you're called a girl but feel you're a boy. You know how boys are treated and what they do. That's how you want to be treated and what you want to do.

Maybe you aren't sure, or don't care that much. Maybe you don't feel like a boy or a girl. Maybe you feel like both. Maybe you just need some time to figure it out, without all the boy and girl stuff.

Because everyone's bodies are different, all our feelings are different too.

Part of being a kid is learning what you like, what you don't like, and who you are. That's part of being a grown-up too. We never stop learning or changing.

Have you noticed that people say that some things are for boys and some are for girls? Have you ever wondered who makes those rules?

Has anyone ever told you that you couldn't do something because you are a boy or a girl?

Look at the activities on these two pages. Which ones do you like to do?

93

Some people say touch is magic.

Touching someone can change the way they feel. Touch can make a hard day a bit easier, a gloomy day a bit brighter, or a lonely day a little less lonely.

Some touch can feel like *helping*.

Touch can help someone feel good, help them get something done they couldn't do on their own, or help them notice something new in the world.

Some touch can feel like *hurting*.

Touch can turn someone from happy to sad. It can make them feel upset or angry.

Everyone feels touch differently. A touch that makes you feel good might make someone else feel bad. The same touch might be welcome one day and unwelcome the next.

One way to show respect and build trust is to ask before you touch someone.

Once you know each other you probably won't ask every time, but with a new person, asking is one way of making your touch help and not hurt.

We all feel touch differently. Only you know what you feel like when you are being touched.

Everyone has times when they want to be touched and other times when they do not want to be touched.

And everyone has times when they change their minds.

Maybe you wanted a hug at first, but then don't feel like a hug—it's okay to say you don't want one.

Maybe you didn't want a hug at first, but then want one after all—it's okay to ask for one.

There are times when someone might have to touch you even if you don't want them to.

Those are helping touches, but they might feel like they hurt.

Whenever anyone touches you and it feels like a hurting touch, it's okay to tell them.

It's also nice to tell people if they are giving you a helping touch and it makes you feel good.

In some families and communities, hugging and kissing is a way of saying hello, showing respect, or showing love.

A parent or family member may expect you to give them, or someone else, a hug or kiss. They may ask you to do this even if you don't want to.

Anytime you are not comfortable touching someone or having someone touch you, you can always try to talk about it.

If you don't feel like hugging or kissing or even shaking hands, there are lots of other ways to show respect or let someone know you care.

106

Touching isn't just something we do with other people. We also touch ourselves.

We touch ourselves all the time, in all kinds of places, for all kinds of reasons.

Touching yourself is one way to learn about yourself, your body, and your feelings.

You may have discovered that touching some parts of your body, especially the middle parts, can make you feel warm and tingly.

Grown-ups call this kind of touch masturbation.

Masturbation is when we touch ourselves, usually our middle parts, to get that warm and tingly feeling.

Every family and community has its own ideas about masturbation.

When you were younger, you may have discovered that it felt good to touch yourself. You may have done this even when you weren't alone.

As you get older, grown-ups expect that if you want to touch yourself to feel good, especially your middle parts, you'll do it when you are in a private place.

You may find that you want some privacy too.

There is another kind of touching that is important to talk about. It is different from all the other kinds of touching in this book. Some people call it secret touching.*

It's called secret touching because no matter where someone touches you or where you touch them, they make you keep it a secret.

They want to keep it a secret because they know that what they are doing is wrong, and they don't want other people to find out.

They might try to scare you so you won't tell. They might be nice to you so you won't tell.

* We learned this from Jan Hindman, who wrote her own book called *A Very Touching Book*. We think Jan and her book are amazing!

Secret touching might be on any part of your body. Usually it's the middle parts, but sometimes it isn't.

Sometimes the person wants to touch you, and sometimes they want you to touch them.

You might not want to tell anyone about it because you think it will get the person in trouble.

If it has been happening for a long time, or it happened a long time ago, it might feel like a secret so big that you have to keep it. But it's not.

You might feel like you did something wrong, but you didn't.

The person who is touching you or asking you to touch them is the one doing something wrong. Secret touching is not your fault. It's never your fault.

If this happens to you, find someone you trust and try to tell them. You can try to tell them what happened, or where it happened, or who it happened with.

If this has already happened to you, or if it happened to a friend or someone you know, it's always good to tell someone, even if it happened a long time ago. Maybe you could tell the person who gave you this book.

The first person you tell might not know what to do, or might not believe you. If that happens, find another person you feel safe and comfortable with and tell them.

The person doing the secret touching might be someone you know. It might be someone in your family, someone you thought you could trust.

Secret touching might feel good like helping touch or bad like hurting touch. It might feel strange or weird or scary, or it may just leave you with questions.

But one way you can tell it's wrong is that the person doing it makes you keep it a secret.

Secret touching isn't like other kinds of secrets. Some secrets, like a birthday present or a surprise, can be fun to have and keep.

But you should never feel like you have to keep a secret when it's about touching. Touching is something you should always be able to talk about.

I THINK TALKING ABOUT SEX IS SEXY!
THERE'S TOO MUCH TALKING IN THIS BOOK. CAN'T WE LEARN WITHOUT TALKING?

KING
SEX
WHAT'S WRONG WITH TALKING ABOUT IT? I FOR ONE APPRECIATE THE OPPORTUNITY FOR AN ADULT DISCUSSION.
WHATEVER.

Some people think there are two kinds of words: *good words* and *bad words*.

A different way to think about it is that words are not good or bad. Words can be helpful, and words can be hurtful.

A word is helpful or hurtful depending on how we use it. It also matters how the word feels to the person we are talking with.

It's like the difference between laughing with someone and laughing at someone.

The same word can feel good, or bad, or like nothing at all. It depends on who is saying it, how they say it, and why.

Some people say sex is a bad word.

Some grown-ups say you should never talk about sex, especially when you are young.

Not everyone feels safe or able to talk about sex. Talking about sex can make some people feel uncomfortable or angry.

But sex isn't a bad word.

It can feel strange to talk about sex if it isn't something you are used to talking about, but strange doesn't mean it's bad or good.

We can ask questions and talk about sex in ways that help and in ways that hurt.

Sexy means different things to different people.

One person may think something or someone is sexy, and another person may not.

When grown-ups call other grown-ups sexy, it usually means they...

think that person looks attractive,

like the way they are dressed,

feel excited by the way they move around.

When grown-ups call themselves sexy, it may mean they...

like how their body feels,

feel good about themselves inside and out,

want to share that feeling with others.

SEXY CAN ALSO BE A FEELING.
SOME PEOPLE THINK THAT SEXY
FEELINGS SHOULD ONLY HAPPEN IN
GROWN-UP RELATIONSHIPS. AND
MANY GROWN-UPS SAY THAT
SEXY IS A WORD TO USE ONLY
WHEN YOU'RE OLDER.

sexy
sexy
sexy
sexy?

WHAT'S FOR SURE IS THAT SEXY IS
A WORD WITH A LOT OF DIFFERENT
MEANINGS, SO IT'S GOOD TO
THINK ABOUT WHAT YOU MEAN
WHEN YOU USE IT.

131

HEY ZAI, IS THERE ANYONE YOU LIKE? YOU KNOW, LIKE REALLY LIKE?
I LIKE MY MOM. I LIKE MY HAMSTER PETE. IS THAT WHAT YOU MEAN?
CRUSHES
RELATI

WHEN I GROW UP I WANT TO MARRY MY PARENTS. THAT WAY WE CAN ALL LIVE TOGETHER FOREVER.
NOT ME—WHEN I GROW UP, I'M GONNA LIVE WITH MY TWO DOGS AND THREE CATS, AND EACH OF US WILL HAVE OUR OWN BEDROOM.
LOVE AND
NSHIPS

134

A crush is a special kind of feeling you have for another person. You can have a crush on any kind of person. You can have a crush on a friend or on someone you just met. You can even have a crush on someone you have never met.

Not everyone has crushes. If you do, the first time can be surprising, and can feel a bit strange.

You don't usually choose to have a crush on someone. It just happens.

You might have a crush on someone who is a lot like you. You might have a crush on someone who is very different from you.

You might think about them a lot. You might want to spend all your time with them if you could.

Just thinking about them can make you happy and nervous. When you are around them, you may feel excited, or awkward, or both.

There's no right or wrong way to have a crush.

For some people, having a crush means wanting to be physically close and touch, like holding hands or hugging.

Other people like to be close but don't want to touch.

Some crushes last a long time, and some are very short.

Sometimes one person has a crush but the other person doesn't.

Other times both people feel the same way.

Some crushes can feel so big that you want to keep them secret. That's your choice. But it's also okay to talk to someone you trust about a crush you have.

You might decide to tell the person you have a crush on, or you might not. It might feel safe to talk about, or not. It will probably depend on how you feel and who the person is.

One more thing to know about crushes: they don't just happen when you are young. People of all ages have crushes.

HAVE YOU EVER HAD A CRUSH ON SOMEONE?

WHAT DID IT FEEL LIKE?

ASK GROWN-UPS YOU TRUST IF THEY HAVE HAD A CRUSH ON SOMEONE.

ASK THEM TO DESCRIBE WHAT IT FELT LIKE.

HAVE A NICE DAY AT WORK, MY LOVE.
SMACK
DAD, WHY DO YOU KISS MOM ON THE LIPS?
WELL . . . ERM . . . BECAUSE WE LOVE EACH OTHER.
I LOVE A LOT OF THINGS BUT I WOULDN'T WANT TO KISS THEM.

Love is another kind of feeling. Like all feelings, it can be hard to describe. Some people think that love is the strongest feeling we can have.

Just like crushes, there are so many different kinds of love.

We can feel love for people in our family. We can feel love for our friends. We can love our pet iguana, or that tree on the street corner.

One love is not better than another. Just like people, every love is different.

As we get older, it can happen that a crush we have turns into love. Sometimes, but not all the time, crushes and love come with sexy feelings.

This may feel grown-up and faraway for you, and it probably is. But it's good to know a little bit about crushes, love, and sexy feelings even before they happen. It's also good to know if you have someone you can trust, in case you have questions.

Love isn't just a feeling we have for other people, places, or things.

We can also love ourselves.

It's nice to try and show ourselves love a little bit every day.

Try and think of one thing you like or love about yourself.

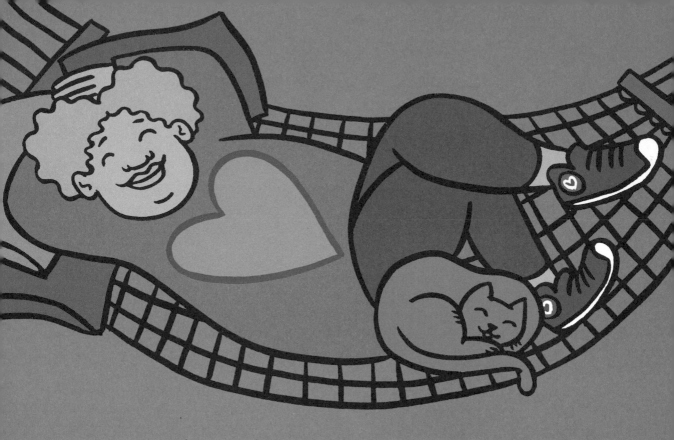

One way to show yourself love and respect is to be nice to your own body. Maybe by taking a rest when you feel tired. Maybe by giving yourself a pat on the back or the arm. Maybe by giving yourself a kiss!

The world can be such a busy place, grown-ups are always asking you to do this and that, be here and there. It can be nice to take a moment every day to say to yourself, "Hi myself! I know I'm not perfect, because no one is, but I am just the way I am."

148

BLOCK PARTY

There are as many different kinds of relationships as there are different kinds of people.

You have relationships with friends, with teachers, with the people who take care of you, with family, and with elders in your community.

You can have imaginary relationships with people you've never met, like someone from a book, movie, or TV show, or someone from your own imagination.

We have some relationships for our whole lives, and some are very short.

When we are young, most of our relationships are with the people we live with, who take care of us. As we get older, we have more choice about who our friends are and who we want to spend time with.

As we get older, some of us decide to start new relationships with people we have a crush on, feel love for, or have sexy feelings for.

Crushes, love, and sexy feelings can happen between people for so many different reasons.

There are lots of different names people use for someone they have a crush on, feel love for, or have sexy feelings for. Here are a few:

You may have noticed that people often talk about relationships between men and women as if those are the only kinds of relationships that can have a crush, love, or sexy feelings. But they aren't.

Have you heard people use the words gay or lesbian? How about asexual or queer?

Those are words people may use to describe themselves, the kinds of relationships they have, and who they have them with. Every community has its own words, but here are a few that lots of people use:

BISEXUAL

GAY

STRAIGHT

LESBIAN

ASEXUAL

QUEER

Some of these words may be new to you. (They may be new to a grown-up you're reading this with too!) If you want to learn more about what they mean, you can look in the back of the book.

Words are important. Like all words, the words we use to describe ourselves and our relationships can be used by others in ways that help us and in ways that hurt us.

It helps when we get to choose what we call ourselves and our relationships.

It helps when we get to choose who we want to have relationships with.

And it helps when every relationship we have includes trust, respect, joy, and justice.

HAS ANYONE EVER USED A WORD TO DESCRIBE YOU IN A WAY THAT HURT?

ASK ADULTS YOU TRUST IF THIS HAS EVER HAPPENED TO THEM.

WHO ARE SOME PEOPLE YOU LIKE?
WHO ARE SOME PEOPLE YOU LOVE?
WHO ARE SOME PEOPLE YOU TRUST?

WHAT THINGS DO YOU THINK ARE IMPORTANT FOR A GOOD RELATIONSHIP?

GLOSSARY!

GLOSSARY? WHAT'S THAT?

Sex isn't the only funny word. You could say all words are funny because what they mean changes over time. And two people may use the same word but mean different things.

Acting with trust, joy, justice, and respect means learning what words mean to other people and trying to use words in ways that feel like they help and not hurt.

Not everyone will agree with the definitions below, but we all need a place to start. If you have a grown-up you can talk to, you might want to ask them what they think these words mean.

By the time you grow up some of the words in this book may mean very different things than what they mean today. The exciting thing to know is that you can be part of that change.

Gay and Lesbian When a man has crushes, love, and/or sexy feelings for other men, he might call himself gay. When a woman has crushes, love, and/or sexy feelings for other women, she might call herself lesbian or gay.

Bisexual When someone has crushes, love, and/or sexy feelings for men and women (and people who are something other than men or women) they might call themselves bisexual.

Straight When men have crushes, love, and/or sexy feelings for women—and when women have crushes, love, and/or sexy feelings for men—they might call themselves straight.

Asexual This is a newer word some people use to describe themselves. When someone doesn't feel sexy feelings for anyone, they might call themselves asexual.

Queer Some people don't feel like any of the words above fit for them. They might not like the rules that other people make for how they feel about themselves and who they have crushes, love, and/or sexy feelings for. Some of those people might call themselves queer.

Puberty A time when your body begins to change faster than it has before. Many of those changes involve your middle parts. It is also a time when how you feel and think, especially about sex, can change. Puberty usually happens over several years, and usually starts sometime between your 8th and your 14th birthday.

Sex When people use the word sex, they usually mean one of three things.

1. Sex is a word that describes our bodies: if someone is called male or female at birth, that is called their sex.

2. Sex describes many different activities that usually involve touching, which people do to feel good in their bodies and to feel close to another person.

3. Sex is a word people use when a person whose body has eggs and a person whose body has sperm come together so that the sperm and egg meet. This is one way that grown-ups can make a baby.

Intersex It's easy to think there are only two options for sex: "male" and "female."

But our bodies are more interesting than that!

Many of us have bodies that aren't considered typically male or female.

The way our middle parts look on the outside, and the way our bodies look and work on the inside, might not fit into the expectations of either male or female bodies. When this happens we call that intersex.

Sometimes this is noticed when a baby is born, and sometimes no one notices until later (usually after puberty). Like all bodies, intersex bodies are different from each other and that is just fine. They aren't wrong or bad.

Gender Nobody agrees on what exactly gender means. Most people would say that gender has something to do with being a boy or a girl. But since there are more than just those two options, gender is always more than that.

Some people say that gender is something we learn. Some people say that gender is something we are born with. Wherever it comes from, and whatever it is, gender is something that people feel on the inside and something we can show on the outside in the way we dress, the way we act, the things we do, and who we like to be friends with. Gender is also something other people will attribute to us, even if we don't agree with it, because of what they think about how we dress, look, and act.

There are lots of different words people use to describe their gender, including words like man, woman, boy, girl, queer, trans, and androgynous. Some Indigenous peoples of North America use the term two-spirit, which is an English word for a very, very old idea that some of us are more than just one thing when it comes to gender.

Trans or Transgender Someone who was called a boy but knows they are a girl—or someone who was called a girl but knows they are a boy—might call themselves trans or transgender as they grow up and learn more about themselves and who they are.

Some people who are called boy or girl—but who don't feel like either of those words fit —might also choose the word transgender.

Some people know this for sure when they are very young, and some people take more time to figure it out.

Gender Diverse, Gender Creative, Gender Non-Conforming, Gender Queer After you are born, sometimes people around you expect you to dress a certain way, make friends with certain people, and want to play in particular ways based on your gender. That works for some kids. But it doesn't work for other kids. Check out the section on Boys, Girls, All of Us if you want to know more about this.

Gender diverse, gender creative, and gender non-conforming are just a few of the terms used to describe kids whose gender doesn't fit with other peoples' expectations.

WHO NEEDS A GLOSSARY? I JUST MAKE UP MY OWN WORDS.

A GLOSSARY IS A LIST OF WORDS WITH EXPLANATIONS OF WHAT EACH WORD MEANS.

159